Easy

PARTY CAKES

Corinne Mitchell

MEREHURST

ACKNOWLEDGEMENTS

I would like to dedicate this book to my
daughters Shula and Kylie.
My special thanks to Jean, Shelley, Karen
and Ian who have helped in so many ways
they are too numerous to list, and to Tim for
all his encouragement and support.

The publishers and author would like to thank
Ian Copping for the photograph used on
page 54; and Anne Smith and Graham Tann
for the photograph on page 44.

Quantities are given in metric, Imperial and cups. Follow one set
of measures as they are not interchangeable.
American terms have been included as necessary throughout,
given in brackets following the UK name.

Published in 1992 by Merehurst Limited, Ferry House,
51–57 Lacy Road, Putney, London SW15 1PR

Copyright © Merehurst Limited 1992

ISBN 1–85391–264–6

A catalogue record of this book is available from the
British Library.

Edited by Barbara Croxford
Designed by Maggie Aldred
Photography by James Duncan

Typeset by J&L Composition Ltd, Filey, North Yorkshire
Colour separation by Fotographics UK – Hong Kong
Printed in Italy by New Interlitho S.p.A

CONTENTS

~

INTRODUCTION

Easy Party Cakes introduces 'Inlaid Icing', a new and exciting technique for creating novelty cakes with a difference. With this technique the design is transferred onto a sugarpasted cake by pricking through tracings made from the templates provided. Each piece of the design is then cut from the cake top and replaced by coloured sugarpaste.

Using this simple technique and easy to use sugarpaste you just can't go wrong, and there's no need to buy expensive equipment – a modelling knife, plastic smoother, pearl/glass head pins and greaseproof (parchment) paper are all you need to get started.

Easy Party Cakes includes six easy to make cake recipes, ranging from a light fresh Orange and Lemon Madeira to a Double Chocolate Treat, with everything in between to tempt all your family and friends.

These outstanding designs have been created to give the maximum effect with minimum work, with all occasions catered for, from a cuddly bear for baby's first birthday to an angel to grace your Christmas table and stylish cakes for men, each with clear step by step instructions and colour photographs.

CORINNE MITCHELL

CAKE RECIPES

CHOCOLATE CHIP AND WALNUT CAKE

Tin (pan) size	15cm (6in) square 18cm (7in) round	18cm (7in) square 20cm (8in) round	20cm (8in) square 23cm (9in) round	23cm (9in) square 25cm (10in) round
Butter	125g (4oz/½ cup)	155g (5oz/⅔ cup)	220g (7oz/⅞ cup)	280g (9oz/scant 1¼ cups)
Soft light brown sugar	90g (3oz/½ cup)	125g (4oz/⅔ cup)	185g (6oz/1 cup)	250g (8oz/1⅓ cups)
Golden (corn) syrup	30ml (2tbsp)	30ml (2tbsp)	45ml (3tbsp)	45ml (3tbsp)
Eggs	2	2	4	5
Self-raising flour	220g (7oz/1¾ cups)	280g (9oz/2¼ cups)	375g (12oz/3 cups)	500g (1lb/4 cups)
Milk	45ml (3tbsp)	60–75ml (4–5tbsp)	75–90ml (5–6tbsp)	75–90ml (5–6tbsp)
Plain (semisweet) chocolate chips or plain cooking chocolate cut into pieces	90g (3oz/¾ cup)	90g (3oz/¾ cup)	125g (4oz/1 cup)	155g (5oz/1¼ cups)
Walnuts, chopped	90g (3oz/¾ cup)	90g (3oz/¾ cup)	125g (4oz/1 cup)	155g (5oz/1¼ cups)
Baking time	50–55mins	1hr 5mins	1hr 10mins	1hr 15mins

1. Preheat the oven to 180°C/350°F/Gas 4.
2. Grease and line the correct size tin (pan).
3. Cream the butter and sugar together in a bowl until light and fluffy.
4. Beat in the syrup.
5. Beat in the eggs, one at a time.
6. Sift the flour and add to the egg mixture, mixing until smooth and creamy.
7. Stir in the milk.
8. Add the chocolate chips and walnuts, stirring until evenly mixed.
9. Turn the mixture into the prepared tin (pan). Bake for the appropriate time or until well risen and a fine skewer inserted into the centre comes out clean.
10. Leave in the tin for 10 minutes, then turn out onto a wire rack to cool.

VARIATIONS

For an all chocolate chip cake, simply omit the walnuts.
    Instead of using walnuts, substitute the same amount of chopped hazelnuts.

NOTE
For a fan assisted oven, check the cake 10 minutes before the end of the stated baking time. This applies to all the cakes.

· TIPS ·

Leave the lining paper on the cake until you are going to prepare the cake for marzipanning as this helps keep the cake moist.

After baking, if not using the cake until the next day, allow to cool and wrap in foil to prevent drying out.

DOUBLE CHOCOLATE TREAT

Tin (pan) size	15cm (6in) square 18cm (7in) round	18cm (7in) square 20cm (8in) round	20cm (8in) square 23cm (9in) round	23cm (9in) square 25cm (10in) round
Self-raising flour	90g (3oz/$\frac{3}{4}$ cup)	185g (6oz/1$\frac{1}{2}$ cups)	280g (9oz/2$\frac{1}{4}$ cups)	375g (12oz/3 cups)
Ground rice	30g (1oz/$\frac{1}{4}$ cup)	60g (2oz/$\frac{1}{3}$ cup)	90g (3oz/$\frac{1}{2}$ cup)	125g (4oz/$\frac{2}{3}$ cup)
Cocoa powder (unsweetened)	60g (2oz/$\frac{1}{2}$ cup)	90g (3oz/$\frac{3}{4}$ cup)	125g (4oz/1 cup)	185g (6oz/1$\frac{1}{2}$ cups)
Butter	125g (4oz/$\frac{1}{2}$ cup)	250g (8oz/1 cup)	375g (12oz/1$\frac{1}{2}$ cups)	500g (1lb/2 cups)
Caster (superfine) sugar	90g (3oz/$\frac{1}{3}$ cup)	185g (6oz/$\frac{3}{4}$ cup)	280g (9oz/1$\frac{1}{4}$ cups)	375g (12oz/1$\frac{1}{2}$ cups)
Vanilla essence	5ml (1tsp)	10ml (2tsp)	15ml (3tsp)	20ml (4tsp)
Eggs, beaten	2	4	5	6
Chocolate chips or plain (semisweet) chocolate cut into small pieces	60g (2oz/$\frac{1}{2}$ cup)	125g (4oz/1 cup)	185g (6oz/1$\frac{1}{2}$ cups)	250g (8oz/2 cups)
Baking time	1hr	1hr 10mins	1hr 15mins	1hr 20mins

1. Preheat the oven to 180°C/350°F/Gas 4.
2. Grease and line the correct size tin (pan).
3. Sift the flour, rice and cocoa together.
4. Cream the butter, sugar and vanilla essence in a bowl until pale and fluffy.
5. Beat in the eggs, a little at a time.
6. Fold in flour, ground rice and cocoa mixture a little at a time, stirring well.
7. Stir in the chocolate chips until evenly mixed.
8. Turn the mixture into the prepared tin (pan). Bake for the appropriate time or until well risen and a fine skewer inserted into the centre comes out clean.
9. Leave in the tin for 10 minutes, then turn onto a wire rack to cool.

QUICK MIX FRUIT CAKE

Tin (pan) size	15cm (6in) square 18cm (7in) round	18cm (7in) square 20cm (8in) round	20cm (8in) square 23cm (9in) round	23cm (9in) square 25cm (10in) round
Butter	185g (6oz/$\frac{3}{4}$ cup)	250g (8oz/1 cup)	315g (10oz/1$\frac{1}{4}$ cups)	375g (12oz/1$\frac{1}{2}$ cups)
Soft light brown sugar	185g (6oz/1 cup)	250g (8oz/1$\frac{1}{3}$ cups)	315g (10oz/1$\frac{2}{3}$ cups)	375g (12oz/2 cups)
Mixed dried fruit	185g (6oz/1 cup)	250g (8oz/1$\frac{1}{3}$ cups)	315g (10oz/1$\frac{2}{3}$ cups)	375g (12oz/2 cups)
Mixed chopped nuts	30g (1oz/$\frac{1}{4}$ cup)	60g (2oz/$\frac{1}{2}$ cup)	125g (4oz/1 cup)	125g (4oz/1 cup)
Glacé (candied) cherries	60g (2oz/$\frac{1}{3}$ cup)	125g (4oz/$\frac{2}{3}$ cup)	185g (6oz/1 cup)	185g (6oz/1 cup)
Self-raising flour, sifted	315g (10oz/2$\frac{1}{2}$ cups)	375g (12oz/3 cups)	500g (1lb/4 cups)	625g (1$\frac{1}{4}$lb/5 cups)
Eggs	3	4	5	6
Ground cinnamon	2.5ml ($\frac{1}{2}$tsp)	2.5ml ($\frac{1}{2}$tsp)	5ml (1tsp)	5ml (1tsp)
Ground mixed spice	2.5ml ($\frac{1}{2}$tsp)	2.5ml ($\frac{1}{2}$tsp)	5ml (1tsp)	5ml (1tsp)
Milk	30ml (2tbsp)	45ml (3tbsp)	60ml (4tbsp)	75ml (5tbsp)
Baking time	1hr 30–35mins	1hr 40–45mins	1hr 50–55mins	1hr 50–55mins

1. Preheat the oven to 180°C/350°F/Gas 4.
2. Grease and line the correct size tin (pan).
3. Place all the ingredients into a large mixing bowl and beat together until well mixed.
4. Turn the mixture into the prepared tin (pan). Bake for the appropriate time or until golden brown and a fine skewer inserted into the centre comes out clean.
5. Leave in the tin for 10 minutes, then turn out onto a wire rack to cool.

· TIP ·

For even distribution of chocolate flavour, it is most important that cocoa powder is well sifted to remove any lumps.

CHERRY AND COCONUT CAKE

Tin (pan) size	15cm (6in) square 18cm (7in) round	18cm (7in) square 20cm (8in) round	20cm (8in) square 23cm (9in) round	23cm (9in) square 25cm (10in) round
Glacé (candied) cherries, quartered	185g (6oz/1 cup)	250g (8oz/1⅓ cups)	250g (8oz/1⅓ cups)	315g (10oz/1⅔ cups)
Desiccated (shredded) coconut	60g (2oz/⅔ cup)	60g (2oz/⅔ cup)	90g (3oz/1 cup)	125g (4oz/1⅓ cups)
Self-raising flour	315g (10oz/2½ cups)	375g (12oz/3 cups)	500g (1lb/4 cups)	625g (1¼lb/5 cups)
Salt	pinch	pinch	1.25ml (¼ tsp)	1.25ml (¼ tsp)
Butter	125g (4oz/½ cup)	185g (6oz/¾ cup)	315g (10oz/1¼ cups)	375g (12oz/1½ cups)
Caster (superfine) sugar	125g (4oz/½ cup)	185g (6oz/¾ cup)	315g (10oz/1¼ cups)	375g (12oz/1½ cups)
Eggs	3	4	5	6
Milk	60–75ml (4–5 tbsp)	75–90ml (5–6 tbsp)	90–105ml (6–7 tbsp)	105–120ml (7–8tbsp)
Baking time	1hr 15mins	1hr 15–20mins	1hr 20–30mins	1hr 25–35mins

1. Preheat the oven to 180°C/350°F/Gas 4.
2. Grease and line the correct size tin (pan).
3. Wash and dry the cherries, then mix with the coconut.
4. Sift the flour and salt into a bowl.
5. Cut the butter into small cubes and rub into the flour until it resembles fine breadcrumbs.
6. Add the sugar, coconut and cherries, stirring lightly to mix.
7. Beat the eggs and milk together, then stir into the mixture.
8. Turn the mixture into the prepared tin (pan). Bake for the appropriate time or until well risen and a fine skewer inserted into the centre comes out clean.
9. Leave in the tin for 10 minutes, then turn out onto a wire rack to cool.

ORANGE AND LEMON MADEIRA

Tin (pan) size	15cm (6in) square 18cm (7in) round	18cm (7in) square 20cm (8in) round	20cm (8in) square 23cm (9in) round	23cm (9in) square 25cm (10in) round
Self-raising flour	185g (6oz/1½ cups)	250g (8oz/2 cups)	315g (10oz/2½ cups)	375g (12oz/3 cups)
Plain (all-purpose) flour	90g (3oz/¾ cup)	125g (4oz/1 cup)	155g (5oz/1¼ cups)	185g (6oz/1½ cups)
Butter	185g (6oz/¾ cup)	250g (8oz/1 cup)	315g (10oz/1¼ cups)	375g (12oz/1½ cups)
Caster (superfine) sugar	185g (6oz/¾ cup)	250g (8oz/1 cup)	315g (10oz/1¼ cups)	375g (12oz/1½ cups)
Eggs	3	4	5	6
Grated orange rind and juice	½	½	½–1	1
Grated lemon rind and juice	½	½	½–1	1
Baking time	1 hr 15 mins	1hr 20mins	1hr 25–30mins	1hr 25–30mins

1. Preheat the oven to 160°C/325°F/Gas 3.
2. Grease and line the correct size tin (pan).
3. Sift the flours together.
4. Cream the butter and sugar together in a bowl until very pale and fluffy.
5. Add one egg plus a spoonful of flour at a time, beating well between each addition.
6. Fold in the remaining flour.
7. Stir in enough orange and lemon juice to give a firm but dropping consistency.
8. Stir in the orange and lemon rind.
9. Turn the mixture into the prepared tin (pan). Bake for the appropriate time or until well risen.
10. Leave in the tin for 10 minutes, then turn out onto a wire rack to cool.

· TIPS ·

The orange and lemon Madeira cake can be frozen for up to six months. Thaw at room temperature while still wrapped.

When a fine skewer inserted into the centre comes out clean, the cake is ready.

PEACH AND PEAR CAKE

Tin (pan) size	15cm (6in) square 18cm (7in) round	18cm (7in) square 20cm (8in) round	20cm (8in) square 23cm (9in) round	23cm (9in) square 25cm (10in) round
Dried ready-to-eat peaches	90g (3oz/⅔ cup)	125g (4oz/¾ cup)	155g (5oz/1 cup)	185g (6oz/1¼ cups)
Dried ready-to-eat pears	90g (3oz/⅔ cup)	125g (4oz/¾ cup)	155g (5oz/1 cup)	185g (6oz/1¼ cups)
Hot boiled water	60ml (2fl oz)	60ml (2fl oz)	90ml (3fl oz)	125ml (4fl oz)
Orange juice	90ml (3fl oz)	90ml (3fl oz)	125ml (4fl oz)	155ml (5fl oz)
Grated orange rind	1	1	1½	2
Butter	125g (4oz/½ cup)	155g (5oz/⅔ cup)	220g (7oz/⅞ cup)	280g (9oz/scant 1¼ cups)
Soft light brown sugar	90g (3oz/½ cup)	125g (4oz/⅔ cup)	185g (6oz/1 cup)	250g (8oz/1⅓ cups)
Clear honey	30ml (2tbsp)	30ml (2tbsp)	45ml (3tbsp)	45ml (3tbsp)
Eggs	2	3	4	5
Self-raising flour	220g (7oz/1¾ cups)	280g (9oz/2¼ cups)	375g (12oz/3 cups)	500g (1lb/4 cups)
Baking time	1hr 10mins	1hr 15mins	1hr 15–20mins	1hr 20–25mins

1. Preheat the oven to 180°C/350°F/Gas 4.
2. Grease and line the correct size tin (pan).
3. Cut the dried fruit into small pieces, place in a bowl and pour over the hot water, orange juice and rind. Leave until cold.
4. Cream the butter and sugar together in a bowl until light and fluffy.
5. Stir in the honey.
6. Beat in the eggs, one at a time.
7. Sift the flour and add to the egg mixture, mixing until smooth and creamy.
8. Fold in the fruit plus soaking juices, stirring until evenly mixed.
9. Turn the mixture into the prepared tin (pan). Bake for the appropriate time or until well risen and a fine skewer inserted into the centre comes out clean.
10. Leave in the tin for 10 minutes, then turn out onto a wire rack to cool.

VARIATIONS

Use any of the dried ready to eat fruits now available, such as apple and apricot, to create your own exciting cake flavours.

NOTE
To soften the dried fruit, it is important to soak them until the water is cold.

· TIPS ·

Grating the rind and squeezing the juice of oranges and lemons is much easier if the fruits are at room temperature.

Wash and dry glacé cherries before tossing in coconut or weighed out flour to prevent them sinking to the bottom of the cake.

COVERING THE CAKE

Covering a Cake with Marzipan

To successfully cover a cake with sugarpaste the edges and corners should be smooth and well rounded, this is achieved by applying the marzipan in one piece. By kneading liquid glycerine (glycerol) into the marzipan it becomes more pliable and easier to work with, which is necessary when applying marzipan this way.

1 Brush a small amount of apricot jam on the centre of the cake board to secure the cake.
2 Level the top of the cake and place upside down on the cake board. If the base edges are not level with the board, make a roll of marzipan to fit the gap, and press into place using a palette knife or a plastic smoother. Fill in any dents and repair any broken corners and edges with marzipan, securing with apricot glaze if necessary.
3 Brush over the cake with apricot glaze.
4 On a surface lightly dusted with icing (confectioner's) sugar, knead the liquid glycerine into the marzipan until smooth and pliable, keeping creases on the underside.
5 Roll out to a thickness of 5mm ($\frac{1}{4}$in) and large enough to cover the whole cake.

6 Using a rolling pin or your hands for support, drape the marzipan over the cake and fan out at the base. Using downward strokes, ease the marzipan to fit the sides without creasing.
7 Trim away the excess at the base with a sharp knife, then use a plastic smoother to remove any dents made whilst working.

Square cake: When covering a square cake, prepare as before. Drape the marzipan over the cake and fan out at the base, cupping your hands to fit the corners carefully ease the marzipan into place. Using downward strokes, press the marzipan against the sides without creasing, then trim away excess at the base with a sharp knife. Use a plastic smoother to remove any dents.

The same 'cupped hand' technique is used when covering a square cake with sugarpaste.

Apricot Glaze

45ml (3tbsp) apricot jam
10ml (2tsp) boiled water

1 Place the apricot jam in a saucepan and heat gently until melted, or heat in a microwave for about 1 minute on High.
2 Remove from the heat and stir in the water. Strain through a sieve to remove the fruit. Allow the glaze to cool before use.

· TIP ·

If you haven't the time to leave the marzipan to dry for 24 hours, roll out the marzipan 2.5 mm ($\frac{1}{8}$in) thick, cover the cake and dust well with icing (confectioner's) sugar. Leave for at least 2 hours. Dust the cake top again with icing sugar, dampen the sides and cover with sugarpaste.

MARZIPAN QUANTITY CHART

Cake size	15cm (6in) square 18cm (7in) round	18cm (7in) square 20cm (8in) round	20cm (8in) square 23cm (9in) round	23cm (9in) square 25cm (10in) round
Marzipan	375g (12oz)	500g (1lb)	750g (1$\frac{1}{2}$lb)	1kg (2lb)
Liquid glycerine (glycerol)	5ml (1tsp)	5ml (1tsp)	7.5ml (1$\frac{1}{2}$ tsp)	10 ml (2tsp)

Covering a Cake with Sugarpaste

When covering a cake with sugarpaste for 'inlaid' decoration, use cooled boiled water to dampen the marzipan on the *sides* of the cake only. This ensures the area on top to be inlaid is kept dry and the cut out sections can be removed easily.

Sugarpaste

Makes 500g (1lb) sugarpaste
45ml (3tbsp) liquid glucose
22.5ml (1½tbsp) powdered gelatine
(unflavored gelatin)
60ml (4tbsp) boiling water
15ml (1tbsp) liquid glycerine (glycerol)
500g (1lb/3½ cups) icing (confectioner's)
sugar
cornflour (cornstarch) for dusting

1 Stand the jar of liquid glucose in a bowl of boiling water for 5–10 minutes to soften. Half-fill a saucepan with water, heat to boiling point, then remove from the heat. Place the gelatine and boiling water in a heatproof bowl over the saucepan of hot water, stir constantly until the gelatine dissolves. Add the liquid glucose and glycerine, then stir until completely blended. Allow to cool for 5 minutes.

2 Sift the icing (confectioner's) sugar into a large mixing bowl and make a well in the centre.

3 Pour the gelatine mixture into the well. Stir with a wooden spoon, gradually drawing in the icing sugar from the side of the bowl, until the mixture becomes stiff and forms a ball.

4 Place the sugarpaste on a surface dusted with cornflour (cornstarch) and knead until smooth, pliable and no longer sticky, dusting the surface with more cornflour if necessary. Store in a polythene bag or cling film (plastic wrap) until needed.

1

On a surface dusted with icing (confectioner's) sugar, knead the sugarpaste until smooth and pliable, keeping the creases on the underside. Roll out the sugarpaste to a thickness of 2.5 mm (⅛in) and large enough to cover the whole cake. Using your hands for support, drape the sugarpaste over the cake.

Although sugarpaste can be made at home, the bought varieties available in most supermarkets are excellent and of a very high standard.

· TIP ·

For a really smooth finish, after rolling out, rub the smoother over the surface of the sugarpaste in a circular motion before draping it over the cake.

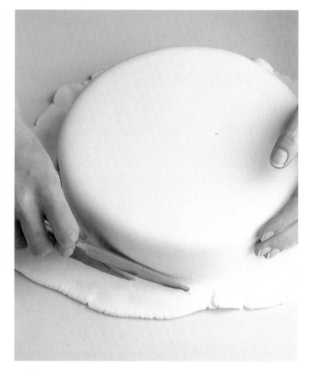

2

Fan out the sugarpaste at the base away from the sides of the cake then, with the palms of your hands and using downward strokes, ease the sugarpaste to fit the sides without creasing.

3

Trim away excess sugarpaste at the base with a sharp knife, then use a plastic smoother to remove any dents. With your hands free from icing (confectioner's) sugar, gently rub over the cake top with circular movements for a smooth and glossy finish.

· TIP ·

For a perfect line around the base of the cake, before cutting away the excess sugarpaste, run the smoother around the sides of the cake. This ensures the sugarpaste is pressed well to the sides at the base and provides a cutting guide.

Colours and Colouring Sugarpaste

Paste colours are ideal for colouring sugarpaste, as it is possible to create both subtle and darker shades without changing the consistency of the sugarpaste. Specialist cake decorating shops carry a wide range of these paste food colours.

Colouring Sugarpaste

Sugarpaste is best coloured in natural light as artificial light can affect colour perception. When this light is not possible, daylight simulation light bulbs can help, these are available from most art and craft shops.

Using a cocktail stick (toothpick), add a small amount of paste colour to the sugarpaste and knead until the colour is even and no longer streaky. Add more colour if needed or more sugarpaste if the colour is too dark. Seal in a polythene bag or cling film (plastic wrap).

Marbling: For a marbled effect, gently knead the colour into the sugarpaste and leave streaky. For subtle marbling only use a small amount of colour or a larger amount for a more dramatic effect (see also page 28).

Mixing Colours

Although there are many colours of paste food colouring available, it is possible to blend two colours together to create another. For this you will need five basic colours only – green (blue in tone), red, yellow, blue (turquoise in tone) and pink. These basic colours can be used in smaller or larger amounts to create both paler and darker shades of the basic colour (see Colour Chart on page 14).

The secondary colours shown on the colour chart are created by blending the colours above and below the basic colours in equal proportions, for example: to mix 125g (4oz) of colour No. 19 pale basic blue + pale basic pink, colour 60g (2oz) sugarpaste pale blue and 60g (2oz) pale pink, then knead the two colours together until completely blended.

Liquid Food Colours

Liquid food colourings can also be used to colour sugarpaste. The liquid food colours available in most major supermarkets are not as rich in colour as those sold in specialist cake decorating shops. It will not be possible to create the darker colours shown on the colour chart with these liquid colours, but pale basic and basic colours can be mixed as above.

If the liquid food colouring you are using does not have a dropper, tip a small amount of the liquid into a bowl and use a teaspoon to add the liquid to the sugarpaste in small amounts. To prevent the sugarpaste from becoming wet and sticky, add the liquid colour one or two drops at a time and knead thoroughly. Should the sugarpaste become sticky, knead in icing (confectioner's) sugar until it returns to a normal consistency.

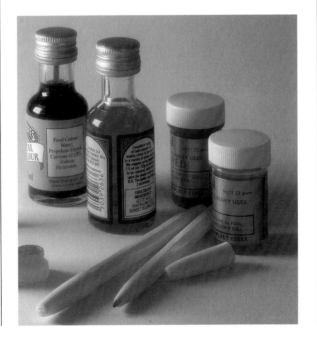

· NOTE ·

Although you need only the basic colours – green, red, yellow, blue and pink – to create all the colours used in these cake designs, there are, of course, a good range of paste colours available. Orange, black, purple and brown are useful extra colours.

When a recipe calls for a colour you do not have, simply refer to the colour chart and mix it yourself!

◀ *Liquid and paste food colours with edible food colour pens.*

13

1 pale basic green
2 basic green
3 dark basic
  green
4 pale basic red
5 basic red
6 basic red +
  dark basic green
7 pale basic red
  + pale basic
  yellow
8 basic red +
  basic yellow +
  white sugarpaste
9 basic red +
  dark yellow
10 pale basic
  yellow
11 basic yellow
12 dark basic
  yellow
13 pale basic
  yellow + pale
  basic blue
14 basic yellow +
  basic blue
15 dark basic
  yellow + dark
  basic blue
16 pale basic blue
17 basic blue
18 dark basic blue
19 pale basic blue
  + pale basic pink
20 basic blue +
  basic pink
21 dark basic blue
  + dark basic pink
22 pale basic pink
23 basic pink
24 dark basic pink

· TIP ·

When you have finished
colouring sugarpaste,
cut the paste in half to
check that the colour is
even and to avoid
streaks or spots.

INLAID ICING TECHNIQUE

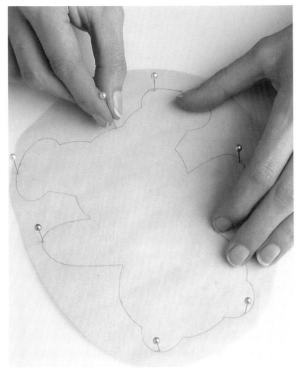

1

Trace the design templates onto sheets of greaseproof (parchment) paper, then trim the paper to fit the cake top. Keeping the areas to be inlaid dry, roll out the sugarpaste to 2.5mm ($\frac{1}{8}$in) and cover the cake.

Position tracing A on the cake top and secure with pearl or glass headed pins on the *inside* edge of the pencil line. Using a pin, mark through the tracing every 2.5mm ($\frac{1}{8}$in) on the *inside* edge of the pencil line, then remove the tracing.

2

Using a modelling knife, cut the section from the sugarpaste, cutting on the *outside* edge of the pin marks. Carefully lift the section from the cake top.

· TIP ·

If you have to leave the cake while in the middle of decorating it, simply cover with cling film (plastic wrap) to prevent the sugarpaste from drying out.

3

Roll out the appropriate coloured sugarpaste to 2.5mm ($\frac{1}{8}$in) on a surface dusted with icing (confectioner's) sugar. Holding the same tracing (A) in position, transfer the design by using a pin to mark through the tracing every 2.5mm ($\frac{1}{8}$in) on the *outside* edge of the pencil line, then remove the tracing.

There will be two lines of marks, the holes that have just been made and dents from the previous transfer. Cut the section out, cutting between the two lines of marks. Lift out the section and inlay into the cake top, using your fingers to smooth over the coloured sugarpaste until the two cut edges meet and the small dents disappear.

4

Using the coloured registration line to ensure the correct position (see page 60), place tracing B on the cake top and secure with pearl or glass headed pins on the *inside* edge of the pencil line. Using a pin, mark through the tracing every 2.5mm ($\frac{1}{8}$in) on the *inside* edge of the pencil line, then remove the tracing.

· TIP ·

Once you have become accustomed to looking at the design in the form of dots, you can save time when transferring the design onto coloured sugarpaste. Lay the tracing onto coloured sugarpaste, then carefully smooth over with your fingers and remove the tracing. An impression from the first pricking will be left on the sugarpaste, carefully cut out the section, cutting on the outside edge of marks.

To check if your coloured sugarpaste is the same thickness as the sugarpaste on the cake, cut a small strip from the edge of the rolled out coloured paste. Take the section that has just been cut from the cake top and lay it along the cut edge. If the coloured sugarpaste is too thin, knead into a ball and roll out again. If it is too thick roll out until the two cut edges match.

5

Roll out the appropriate coloured sugarpaste to 2.5mm ($\frac{1}{8}$in) on a surface dusted with icing (confectioner's) sugar. Hold tracing B in position, using a pin, mark through the tracing every 2.5mm ($\frac{1}{8}$in) on the *outside* edge of the pencil line. Cut each section of the design from the cake top and inlay with the appropriate coloured section, using your fingers to smooth over the coloured sugarpaste until the two cut edges meet and the small dents disappear. Only cut out and inlay one section at a time.

When all the sections have been completed, gently smooth over the cake top with a plastic smoother to remove any dents made whilst working.

6

Repeat the procedure for tracings C and D as the design requires, using the coloured registration line to ensure the correct position. When all the sections have been completed, lightly dust the cake top with icing (confectioner's) sugar and use a plastic smoother to remove any dents.

If the sugarpaste appears dry or cracked from the icing sugar, cover with cling film (plastic wrap) for 2–3 hours until the icing sugar has been absorbed.

· NOTE ·

Adding features and line decorations

Facial features, greetings and other decorative lines can be painted or drawn onto a cake using paste food colour or edible food colour pens.

Trace the feature(s) required onto greaseproof (parchment) paper then, using a coloured crayon, trace the surrounding main outline to use as a registration line. When the sugarpaste is dry, place the tracing on the cake top using the registration line to ensure the correct position. Retrace over the pencil lines, then remove the tracing.

Draw over the *impression* left in the sugarpaste with appropriate coloured edible food colour pen or paint over using a fine paint brush and paste food colour. (See also page 26.)

CUDDLES

This charming teddy bear cake for a young child is also featured on pages 15–17. If necessary, the number on the bear's tummy can be altered to the appropriate age (see page 80).

18cm (7in) or 20cm (8in) round or square cake of your choice, see pages 6–9

•

marzipan to cover cake

•

750g (1½lb) sugarpaste

•

yellow, brown and red paste food colours

•

icing (confectioner's) sugar to dust

•

brown edible food colour pen

•

ribbon and candles to decorate, optional

1 Cover the cake with marzipan, see page 10, then allow to dry in a warm place for 24 hours. Trace the templates from page 60 onto greaseproof (parchment) paper, then trim the paper to fit the cake top.

2 Colour 185g (6oz) sugarpaste yellow, 15g (½oz) brown and 30g (1oz) red, keep aside 15g (½oz) white. Roll out the remaining sugarpaste to 2.5mm (⅛in) and cover the cake, see pages 11–12.

3 Secure tracing A (teddy) in position on the cake top, transfer the design then remove the tracing. Cut out the teddy and inlay with yellow sugarpaste.

4 Secure tracing B (tummy, face and paws) in position, transfer the design then remove the tracing. Cut out the tummy and inlay with white sugarpaste. Cut out the facial features and inlay with brown sugarpaste. Cut out the paws and inlay with brown sugarpaste.

5 Secure tracing C (number and bow) in position, transfer the design then remove the tracing. Cut out the number and inlay with red sugarpaste. Cut out the bow and inlay with red sugarpaste.

6 Lightly dust the cake top with icing (confectioner's) sugar and use a smoother to remove any dents. Allow the sugarpaste to dry for 24–48 hours or until completely dry and will not dent when pressed.

7 Trace teddy's mouth onto greaseproof paper, then using a coloured crayon trace the outline of teddy's nose and eyes to use as a registration line. Hold the tracing in position on the cake top, pressing gently, carefully re-trace over the pencil lines then remove the tracing. Use the brown edible food colour pen to draw in teddy's mouth from the impression left (see also page 26). Decorate with ribbon and candles if using.

Inlaying teddy (tracing A) in yellow sugarpaste.

· TIP ·

To save time when cutting out small paw sections, use the head of a pin to make small dents, then fill with small balls of brown sugarpaste.

HETTY, BETTY AND BABY BOO

A pretty cake for a little birthday boy or girl. As with all the cakes, this design can be personalized by adding an appropriate number of candles and coloured ribbon.

20cm (8in) or 23cm (9in) square cake of your choice, see pages 6–9

•

marzipan to cover cake

•

750g (1½lb) sugarpaste

•

black, pink and blue paste food colours

•

icing (confectioner's) sugar to dust

•

ribbon and candles to decorate, optional

1 Cover the cake with marzipan, see page 10, then allow to dry in a warm place for 24 hours. Trace the templates from page 61 onto greaseproof (parchment) paper, then trim the paper to fit the cake top.

2 Colour 125g (4oz) sugarpaste grey, 60g (2oz) pink and 60g (2oz) blue. Roll out the remaining sugarpaste to 2.5mm (⅛in) and cover the cake, see pages 11–12.

3 Secure tracing A (elephants and balloons) in position on the cake top, transfer the design then remove the tracing. Cut out the elephants and inlay with grey sugarpaste. Cut out the balloons and inlay one with pink sugarpaste and the other with blue sugarpaste.

4 Secure tracing B (blankets) in position,

transfer the design then remove the tracing. Cut out the large blankets and inlay with pink sugarpaste. Cut out the small blanket and inlay with blue sugarpaste.

5 Hold tracing C (spots and balloon strings) in position, transfer the design then remove the tracing. Cut out the spots on the pink blankets and inlay with blue sugarpaste. Cut out the spot on the blue blanket and inlay with pink sugarpaste. Cut out the balloon strings and inlay with pink and blue sugarpaste.

6 Using a cocktail stick (toothpick) make small dents for the elephants' eyes and fill with small balls of blue sugarpaste.

7 Lightly dust the cake top with icing (confectioner's) sugar and use a smoother to remove any dents. Decorate with ribbon and candles.

· TIP ·

When inlaying the balloon strings, use the edge of a knife blade to ease the sugarpaste into position.

To save time when filling small circular sections, make small balls of appropriate coloured sugarpaste, then gently press into place and smooth over.

BRULEE

This friendly dog will delight both children and dog-lovers alike. Vary the colour of the dog if liked so the cake relates to a special pet.

20cm (8in) or 23cm (9in) square cake of your choice, see pages 6–9

•

marzipan to cover cake

•

875g (1¾lb) sugarpaste

•

blue, black and red paste food colours

•

icing (confectioner's) sugar to dust

•

ribbon and candles to decorate, optional

1 Cover the cake with marzipan, see page 10, then allow to dry in a warm place for 24 hours. Trace the templates from page 62 onto grease-proof (parchment) paper, then trim the paper to fit the cake top.

2 Colour 220g (7oz) sugarpaste blue, 125g (4oz) black, 7g (¼oz) red and set aside 100g (3½oz) white. Roll out the remaining sugarpaste to 2.5mm (⅛in) and cover the cake, see pages 11–12.

3 Secure the inset tracing in position on the cake top, transfer the inset outline then remove the tracing. Cut out the inset and inlay with blue sugarpaste.

4 Secure tracing A (body and ears) in position, transfer the design then remove the tracing. Cut out the body and inlay with black sugarpaste. Cut out the ears and inlay with white sugarpaste.

5 Secure tracing B (bib, face and tongue) in position, transfer the design then remove the tracing. Cut out the bib and inlay with white sugarpaste. Cut out the face and inlay with white sugarpaste. Cut out the tongue and inlay with red sugarpaste.

6 Hold tracing C (eyes and nose) in position, transfer the design then remove the tracing. Cut out the eyes and inlay with blue sugarpaste. Cut out the nose and inlay with black sugarpaste.

7 Hold tracing D (eye centres) in position, transfer the design then remove the tracing. Cut out the eye centres and inlay with black sugarpaste.

8 Lightly dust the cake top with icing (confectioner's) sugar and use a smoother to remove any dents. Decorate with ribbon and candles if using.

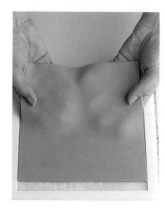

Starting at the top edge, lay the coloured inset into place, then using your hands smooth outwards from the centre until all the cut edges meet. Use a plastic smoother to remove any dents.

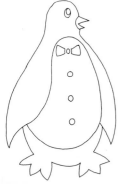

Carefully lift the blue sugarpaste onto the cake top, matching the two cut edges together, then ease the sugarpaste to fit the cake corners and sides. Trim away the excess at the base with a sharp knife and use a smoother to remove any dents.

· TIP ·

Using a pin head, make small dents for buttons and bow tie centres, then fill with small balls of black sugarpaste. For small areas, this is a quick alternative method.

CUTHBERT

Instead of a white sugarpaste background, this cake is covered in two colours with stunning results.

20cm (8in) or 23cm (9in) square cake of your choice, see pages 6–9

•

marzipan to cover cake

•

1kg (2lb) sugarpaste

•

blue, black and orange paste food colours

•

icing (confectioner's) sugar to dust

•

ribbon and candles to decorate, optional

1 Cover the cake with marzipan, see page 10, then allow to dry in a warm place for 24 hours. Trace the templates from page 63 onto grease-proof (parchment) paper, then trim the paper to fit the cake top.
2 Colour 375g (12oz) sugarpaste blue, 155g (5oz) black, 90g (3oz) orange and set aside 7g (¼oz) white. Roll out the remaining sugarpaste to 2.5mm (⅛in) and cover the cake up to the back top edge only, taking care to only dampen the front and half way along the sides of the cake with cooled boiled water.
3 Secure tracing A (mountain) in position on the cake top so the highest point of mountain falls 2cm (¾in) below the back edge of the cake, and the design continues down both sides of the cake. Transfer the design then remove the tracing. Cut along the mountain edge and remove trimmings.
4 Roll out the blue sugarpaste to 2.5mm (⅛in) and large enough to cover the top half and sides of the cake. Keeping the sugarpaste on a

flat surface, trim to give a straight edge. Hold tracing A in position so the blue sugarpaste extends 2cm (¾in) plus depth of side, beyond the highest point of mountain. Transfer the design then remove the tracing. Cut along the mountain outline and remove trimmings. Dampen the top half of the cake sides and back side with cooled boiled water. Using your hands or a rolling pin for support, carefully lift the blue sugarpaste onto the cake, matching the two cut edges together. Smooth the sugarpaste down the sides and back edge of the cake, then trim away excess at the base with a sharp knife. Use a smoother to remove any dents.
5 Secure tracing B (Cuthbert, moon and hat) in position, transfer the design then remove the tracing. Cut out Cuthbert and inlay with black sugarpaste. Cut out the feet and inlay with orange sugarpaste. Cut out the moon and inlay with white sugarpaste. Cut out the hat and inlay with black sugarpaste.
6 Secure tracing C (bow ties, buttons, eyes, beak and hat band) in position, transfer the design then remove the tracing. Cut out the bow ties and inlay with black sugarpaste. Cut out the buttons and inlay with black sugarpaste. Cut out Cuthbert's eye and inlay with white sugarpaste. Cut out the moon's eye and inlay with orange sugarpaste. Cut out the hat band and inlay with orange sugarpaste.
7 Using a cocktail stick (toothpick) make dents for the centre eyes, then fill with small balls of black sugarpaste. Lightly dust the cake top with icing (confectioner's) sugar and use a smoother to remove any dents.

JASPER'S FRIEND

The stripey cat's face is drawn on using a simple tracing technique and an edible food colour pen.

Using the coloured registration line to ensure the correct position, place the tracing of Jasper's nose and whiskers on the cake top. Retrace over the nose and whiskers then remove the tracing. Draw over the impression left in sugarpaste with black edible food colour pen.

18cm (7in) or 20cm (8in) round cake of your choice, see pages 6–9

•

marzipan to cover cake

•

750g (1½lb) sugarpaste

•

orange, black, green and blue paste food colours

•

icing (confectioner's) sugar to dust

•

black edible food colour pen

•

ribbons and candles to decorate, optional

1 Cover the cake with marzipan, see page 10, then allow to dry in a warm place for 24 hours. Trace the templates from page 64 on to grease-proof (parchment) paper, then trim the paper to fit the cake top.

2 Colour 125g (4oz) sugarpaste orange, 90g (3oz) black, 30g (1oz) green and marble 30g (1oz) with blue (see pages 13 and 28). Roll out the remaining sugarpaste to 2.5mm (⅛in) and cover the cake, see pages 11–12.

3 Secure tracing A (cat and fish bowl) in position on the cake top, transfer the design then remove the tracing. Cut out the cat and inlay with orange sugarpaste. Cut out the fish bowl and inlay with the marbled sugarpaste.

4 Secure tracing B (fish, fins, fish tail and leaves) in position, transfer the design then remove the tracing. Cut out the fish and inlay with orange sugarpaste. Cut out the fins and

inlay with black sugarpaste. Cut out the tail and inlay with black sugarpaste. Cut out the leaves and inlay with green sugarpaste.

5 Secure tracing C (cat's stripes and eyes and fish's eye) in position, transfer the design then remove the tracing. Starting on the cat's head and working downwards, cut out and inlay each stripe with black sugarpaste. Cut out the cat's eyes and inlay with green sugarpaste. Cut out the fish's eye and inlay with green sugarpaste.

6 Hold tracing D (cat's middle and centre eyes) in position, transfer the design then remove the tracing. Cut out the middle eye and inlay with black sugarpaste. Cut out the centre eye and inlay with green sugarpaste.

7 Using a pin head, make a small dent in the top half of fish's eye and fill with a small ball of black sugarpaste. Make small dents in the fish bowl to resemble air bubbles and fill with small balls of white sugarpaste.

8 Lightly dust the cake top with icing (confectioner's) sugar and use a smoother to remove any dents. Allow the sugarpaste to dry for 24–48 hours or until completely dry and will not dent when pressed.

9 Trace the cat's facial features onto grease-proof paper, then using a coloured crayon trace the outline of cat's head and eyes to use as a registration line. Hold the tracing in position on the cake top, pressing gently, carefully re-trace over the pencil lines then remove the tracing. Use the black edible food colour pen to draw in the facial features. Decorate with ribbons and candles if using.

DINO

A jolly dinosaur and a seven-year-old make
the perfect partners. Of course, you can
substitute any number for the age required
(see page 80).

*20cm (8in) or 23cm (9in) square cake of
your choice, see pages 6–9*

•

marzipan to cover cake

•

1kg (2lb) sugarpaste

•

yellow, green and orange paste food colours

•

icing (confectioner's) sugar to dust

•

ribbon and candles to decorate, optional

1 Cover the cake with marzipan, see page 10,
then allow to dry in a warm place for 24 hours.
Trace the templates from page 65 onto grease-
proof (parchment) paper, then trim the paper
to fit the cake top.

2 Colour 185g (6oz) sugarpaste yellow then
marble with green paste food colour, colour
185g (6oz) orange. Roll out the remaining
sugarpaste to 2.5mm (⅛in) and cover the cake,
see pages 11–12.

3 Secure tracing A (number 7) in position on
the cake top, transfer the design then remove
the tracing. Cut out the number 7 and inlay
with orange sugarpaste.

4 Secure tracing B (Dino) in position, transfer
the design then remove the tracing. Cut out
Dino and inlay with marbled sugarpaste.

5 Hold tracing C (teeth and eye) in position,
transfer the design then remove the tracing.
Cut out the teeth and inlay with white sugarpaste. Cut out the eye and inlay with orange

sugarpaste. Using a pin head, make a dent in
eye centre and fill with a ball of marbled
sugarpaste.

6 Lightly dust the cake top with icing (confectioner's) sugar and use a smoother to remove
any dents. Decorate with ribbon and candles if
using.

Colour the sugarpaste
yellow then add green
paste food colour on a
cocktail stick
(toothpick). Fold the
sugarpaste up and roll
between the hands,
twisting and turning to
create a marbled effect,
adding more colour if
necessary.

· TIP ·

Using your hands to
support Dino's head
and body, place the
points, feet and tail into
position first, then
guide the remaining
sections into place
working upwards
towards the head.

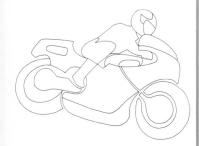

TURBO CHARGER

A stunning motorbike design for a young man. The colours can be altered to match a particular bike (see the colour chart on page 14).

23cm (9in) square cake of your choice, see pages 6–9

•

marzipan to cover cake

•

1kg (2lb) sugarpaste

•

red, yellow, black and blue paste food colours

•

icing (confectioner's) sugar to dust

•

ribbon and candles to decorate, optional

1 Cover the cake with marzipan, see page 10, then allow to dry in a warm place for 24 hours. Trace the templates from page 66 onto grease-proof (parchment) paper, then trim the paper to fit the cake top.

2 Colour 125g (4oz) sugarpaste red, 60g (2oz) yellow, 60g (2oz) grey, 30g (1oz) light blue and 30g (1oz) dark blue. Roll out the remaining sugarpaste to 2.5mm ($\frac{1}{8}$in) and cover the cake, see pages 11–12.

3 Secure tracing A (bike and wheels) in position on the cake top, transfer the design then remove the tracing. Cut out the bike sections and inlay with red sugarpaste. Cut out the small bike sections and inlay with yellow sugarpaste. Cut out the wheels and inlay with grey sugarpaste.

4 Secure tracing B (rider, centre wheels, petrol tank, bike detail) in position, transfer the design then remove the tracing. Cut out the boot and inlay with grey sugarpaste. Cut out the leg and inlay with light blue sugarpaste. Cut out the body and inlay with dark blue sugarpaste. Cut out the helmet and inlay with red sugarpaste. Cut out the visor and inlay with grey sugarpaste. Cut out the petrol tank and inlay with yellow sugarpaste. Cut out the centre wheels and inlay with yellow sugarpaste. Cut out the bike detail and inlay with white sugarpaste.

5 Hold tracing C (flash on helmet) in position, transfer the design then remove the tracing. Cut out the flash and inlay with pale blue sugarpaste.

6 Lightly dust the cake top with icing (confectioner's) sugar and use a smoother to remove any dents. Decorate with ribbon and candles if using.

When all the sections have been completed, lightly dust cake top with icing (confectioner's) sugar and use a plastic smoother to remove any dents.

TROJAN CLOUD

Making a very effective use of marbled sugarpaste, here is a celebration cake perfect for a horse-lover. This dramatic design is one of the easiest to do!

23cm (9in) square cake of your choice, see pages 6–9

•

marzipan to cover cake

•

750g (1½lb) sugarpaste

•

black paste food colour

•

icing (confectioner's) sugar to dust

•

ribbon and candles to decorate, optional

1 Cover the cake with marzipan, see page 10, then allow to dry in a warm place for 24 hours. Trace the templates from page 67 onto grease-proof (parchment) paper, then trim the paper to fit the cake top.
2 Marble 220g (7oz) sugarpaste grey using black paste food colour (see pages 13 and 28) and colour 30g (1oz) sugarpaste black. Roll out the remaining sugarpaste to 2.5mm (⅛in) and cover the cake, see pages 11–12.
3 Secure tracing A (horse and horse-shoe) in position on the cake top, transfer the design then remove the tracing. Cut out the horse-shoe and inlay with marbled sugarpaste. Cut out the horse and inlay with marbled sugar-paste. Cut out the mane and inlay with black sugarpaste. Cut out the tail and inlay with black sugarpaste.
4 Secure tracing B (horse-shoe nails) in position, transfer the design then remove the tracing. Cut out the nails and inlay with black sugarpaste.

5 Lightly dust the cake top with icing (confectioner's) sugar and use a smoother to remove any dents. Decorate with ribbon and candles if using.

Supporting the horse-shoe with your hands, lay it in position on the cake top easing the top edges and corners into place first, then lay the curved section into place. Smooth over until the cut edges meet.

· TIP ·

If making this cake for a child, choosing bright colours for the horse and horse-shoe will give the cake a completely different look.

CASTAWAY

A colourful cake to remind you of a holiday,
the sea and the sun. This cake also makes
the perfect choice as a 'Bon voyage' send off.

*20cm (8in) square cake of your choice, see
pages 6–9*

•

marzipan to cover cake

•

750g (1½lb) sugarpaste

•

*orange, yellow, green and blue paste food
colours*

•

icing (confectioner's) sugar to dust

•

ribbon and candles to decorate, optional

1 Cover the cake with marzipan, see page 10,
then allow to dry in a warm place for 24 hours.
Trace the templates from page 68 onto grease-
proof (parchment) paper, then trim the paper
to fit the cake top.
2 Colour 60g (2oz) sugarpaste orange, 90g
(3oz) yellow, 125g (4oz) green and 30g (1oz)
blue. Roll out the remaining sugarpaste to
2.5mm (⅛in) and cover the cake, see pages
11–12.
3 Secure tracing A (boat and sun) in position
on the cake top, transfer the design then remove the tracing. Cut out the sun and inlay
with orange sugarpaste. Cut out the boat and
inlay with orange sugarpaste. Cut out the flag
and inlay with orange sugarpaste. Cut out the
sails and inlay with yellow sugarpaste.
4 Secure tracing B (palm tree and waves) in
position, transfer the design then remove the
tracing. Cut out the palms and inlay with green
sugarpaste. Cut out the coconuts and inlay

with orange sugarpaste. Cut out the tree trunk
and inlay with yellow sugarpaste. Cut out the
waves and inlay with blue sugarpaste.
5 Lightly dust the cake top with icing (confectioner's) sugar and use a smoother to remove
any dents. Decorate with ribbon and candles if
using.

As the design is
gradually built up
you can see how
effective cutting
through the different
colours becomes.

· TIP ·

To save time when
filling small circular
sections, such as the
coconuts, make small
balls of sugarpaste and
press gently into the cut
out spaces. Smooth
over well.

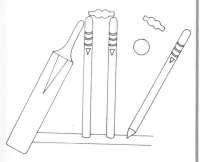

BOWLED OUT

Sport cakes are always popular with
boys and men, and this cricket cake is
no exception.

*20cm (8in) square cake of your choice, see
pages 6–9*

•

marzipan to cover cake

•

875g (1¾lb) sugarpaste

•

green, yellow and red paste food colours

•

icing (confectioner's) sugar

•

ribbon and candles to decorate, optional

· TIPS ·

If the coloured
sugarpaste appears
patchy or dry from
using icing
(confectioner's) sugar,
cover with cling film
(plastic wrap) for 1–2
hours or until all the
icing sugar has been
absorbed.

~

For an easy square cake
top inset, see the tip on
page 22.

1 Cover the cake with marzipan, see page 10,
then allow to dry in a warm place for 24 hours.
Trace the templates from page 69 onto grease-
proof (parchment) paper, then trim the paper
to fit the cake top.
2 Colour 185g (6oz) sugarpaste green, 90g
(3oz) yellow, 30g (1oz) red and set aside 60g
(2oz) white. Roll out the remaining sugarpaste
to 2.5mm (⅛in) and cover the cake, see pages
11–12.
3 Secure the inset tracing on the cake top,
transfer the inset outline then remove the tracing. Cut out the inset and inlay with green.
4 Secure tracing A (white batting crease) in
position, transfer the design then remove the
tracing. Cut out the batting crease and inlay
with white sugarpaste.
5 Secure tracing B (bat, stumps and ball) in
position, transfer the design then remove the
tracing. Cut out the bat and inlay with yellow
sugarpaste. Cut out the stumps and inlay with
yellow. Cut out the ball and inlay with red.

6 Secure tracing C (bat handle, stump pattern
and bails) in position, transfer the design then
remove the tracing. Cut out the handle and
inlay with red sugarpaste. Cut out the pattern
on the stumps and inlay with red sugarpaste.
Cut out the bails and inlay with yellow.
7 Using a modelling knife, make three cuts
across each stump then make small cuts across
the ball to form a stitch pattern. Rub over with
icing (confectioner's) sugar to fill.
8 Lightly dust the cake top with icing sugar
and use a smoother to remove any dents.

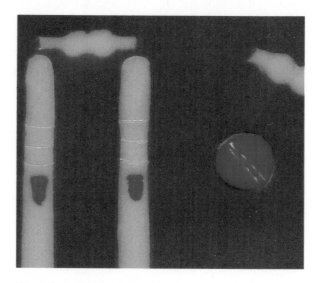

The white lines on the
stumps are made by
making three cuts into
the yellow sugarpaste,
then rubbing icing
(confectioner's) sugar
into them to fill.

FA CUP

A dramatic-looking cake for the football enthusiast. For the younger person, why not include their age in the design. Simply trace the appropriate number (see page 80) and use it as tracing D in the centre of the cup.

18cm (7in) or 20cm (8in) round or hexagonal cake of your choice, see pages 6–9

•

marzipan to cover cake

•

685g (1lb 6oz) sugarpaste

•

black and yellow paste food colours

•

icing (confectioner's) sugar to dust

•

ribbons and candles to decorate, optional

· TIPS ·

Mark through the tracing at the pentagon corners only, then line up the pin marks with a metal ruler and cut out. Repeat on the coloured sugarpaste.

If the black sugarpaste appears patchy or dry from using icing (confectioner's) sugar, cover with cling film (plastic wrap) for 1–2 hours or until all the icing sugar has been absorbed.

1 Cover the cake with marzipan, see page 10, then allow to dry in a warm place for 24 hours. Trace the templates from page 70 onto greaseproof (parchment) paper, then trim the paper to fit the cake top.

2 Colour 125g (4oz) sugarpaste black and 60g (2oz) yellow. Roll out the remaining sugarpaste to 2.5mm (⅛in) and cover the cake, see pages 11–12.

3 Secure tracing A (pentagon) in position on the cake top, transfer the design then remove the tracing. Cut out the pentagon and inlay with black sugarpaste.

4 Secure tracing B (cup) in position, transfer the design then remove the tracing. Cut out the cup and inlay with yellow sugarpaste.

5 Hold tracing C (cup handles) in position, transfer the design then remove the tracing. Cut out the handles and inlay with black sugarpaste.

6 Lightly dust the cake top with icing (confectioner's) sugar and use a smoother to remove any dents. Decorate with ribbon and candles if using.

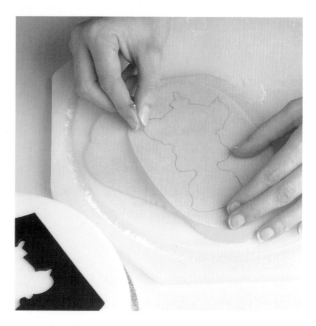

Roll out yellow sugarpaste to 2.5mm (⅛in) then place tracing B in position. Using a pin, mark through tracing on the outside edge of the pencil line every 2.5mm (⅛in), then cut out between the two lines of marks and inlay onto the cake top. Use a smoother to remove any dents.

BOYS' TOY

The ideal birthday or celebration cake for
'boys' of all ages!

*20cm (8in) square cake of your choice, see
pages 6–9*

•

marzipan to cover cake

•

1kg (2lb) sugarpaste

•

red and black paste food colours

•

icing (confectioner's) sugar to dust

•

ribbon and candles to decorate, optional

1 Cover the cake with marzipan, see page 10, then allow to dry in a warm place for 24 hours. Trace the templates from page 71 onto grease-proof (parchment) paper, then trim the paper to fit the cake top.

2 Colour 185g (6oz) sugarpaste red, 60g (2oz) grey, set aside 185g (6oz) white, then colour the remaining sugarpaste black. Roll out the black sugarpaste to 2.5mm ($\frac{1}{8}$in) and cover the cake, see pages 11–12.

3 Secure the inset tracing in position on the cake top, transfer the inset outline then remove the tracing. Cut out the inset and inlay with white sugarpaste.

4 Secure tracing A (corner triangles and stripes) in position on the cake top, transfer the design then remove the tracing. Cut out the triangles and inlay with red sugarpaste. Cut out the stripes and inlay with red sugarpaste.

5 Secure tracing B (car, sills, wheels and spoiler) in position, transfer the design then remove the tracing. Cut out the car and inlay with red sugarpaste. Cut out the sills and inlay with grey sugarpaste. Cut out the wheels and inlay with grey sugarpaste. Cut out the spoiler and inlay with grey sugarpaste.

6 Secure tracing C (windows, car details, centre wheels and stripes) in position, transfer the design then remove the tracing. Cut out the windows and inlay with grey sugarpaste. Cut out the car details and inlay with grey sugarpaste. Cut out the centre wheels and inlay with black sugarpaste. Cut out the stripes and inlay with black sugarpaste.

7 Lightly dust the cake top with icing (confectioner's) sugar and use a smoother to remove any dents. Decorate with ribbon and candles if using.

Cut out the corner
triangle and inlay with
red sugarpaste, then cut
out the stripe and inlay
with red sugarpaste.
Repeat in the opposite
corner.

· TIPS ·

When cutting out the cake top inlay and corner design, mark the corner points only, then line up the pin marks with a metal ruler and cut out. Repeat on the coloured sugarpaste.

If the black sugarpaste appears patchy or dry from using icing (confectioner's) sugar, cover with cling film (plastic wrap) for 1–2 hours or until all the icing sugar has been absorbed.

TEE OFF

A spectacular cake to impress a golfer. A
pearl or glass headed pin was used to make
the realistic marks on the golf ball.

*18cm (7in) or 20cm (8in) round cake of
your choice, see pages 6–9*

•

marzipan to cover cake

•

750g (1½lb) sugarpaste

•

*green, yellow, red and black paste food
colours*

•

icing (confectioner's) sugar to dust

•

ribbon and candles to decorate, optional

1 Cover the cake with marzipan, see page 10,
then allow to dry in a warm place for 24 hours.
Trace the templates from page 72 onto grease-
proof (parchment) paper, then trim the paper
to fit the cake top.
2 Colour 470g (15oz) sugarpaste light green,
60g (2oz) yellow, 45g (1½oz) red, 30g (1oz)
grey and 30g (1oz) dark green, set aside 100g
(3½oz) white. Roll out the light green sugarpaste to 2.5mm (⅛in) and cover the cake, see
pages 11–12.
3 Secure the inset tracing in position on the
cake top, transfer the inset outline then remove
the tracing. Cut out the inset and inlay with
white sugarpaste.
4 Secure tracing A (flag, tee, club, ball and
grass) in position on the cake top, transfer the
design then remove the tracing. Cut out the flag
and inlay with red sugarpaste. Cut out the tee
and inlay with red sugarpaste. Cut out the
club and inlay with grey sugarpaste. Cut out the

ball and inlay with yellow sugarpaste. Cut out
the grass and inlay with dark green sugarpaste.
5 Secure tracing B (club inset and pole) in
position, transfer the design then remove the
tracing. Cut out the club inset and inlay with
yellow sugarpaste. Cut out the pole sections
one at a time and inlay alternately with yellow
and dark green sugarpaste.
6 Hold tracing C (pattern on club) in position, transfer the design then remove the
tracing. Cut out the bars and inlay with grey
sugarpaste. Using the head of a pin make
shallow dents in the golf ball.
7 Lightly dust the cake top with icing (confectioner's) sugar and use a smoother to remove
any dents.

The golf ball is made to
look so lifelike by
simply pressing the top
of a pearl or glass
headed pin into the
yellow sugarpaste.

· TIP ·

If you have a tin lid
approximately the
same size as the inset,
use it to cut out the
inset from the cake top
instead of using the
inset tracing. Repeat on
the coloured sugarpaste.

SPRING BOUQUET

The pretty flower design is perfect for a birthday celebration or Mother's Day cake and can be carried out in any colours of your choice; select from the colour chart on page 14.

18cm (7in) or 20cm (8in) round cake of your choice, see pages 6–9

•

marzipan to cover cake

•

875g (1¾lb) sugarpaste

•

purple, pink, blue, yellow and green paste food colours

•

icing (confectioner's) sugar to dust

•

ribbon and candles to decorate, optional

1 Cover the cake with marzipan, see page 10, then allow to dry in a warm place for 24 hours. Trace the template from page 73 onto grease-proof (parchment) paper, then trim the paper to fit the cake top.

2 Colour 125g (4oz) sugarpaste lilac, 60g (2oz) pale pink, 15g (½oz) blue, 30g (1oz) yellow, 45g (1½oz) pale green and 15g (½oz) dark green. Roll out the remaining sugarpaste to 2.5mm (⅛in) and cover the cake, see pages 11–12.

3 Secure the tracing in position on the cake top, transfer the design then remove the tracing. Cut out and inlay each section with the appropriate coloured sugarpaste, see the finished cake photograph for colour guide.

4 Lightly dust the cake top with icing (confectioner's) sugar and use a smoother to remove any dents. Decorate with ribbon and candles if using.

· TIP ·

Regularly clean the modelling knife or scalpel blade with a damp cloth to ensure clean sharp cuts.

1 Always colour sugarpaste in natural light, as artificial light can affect colour perception.

2 Add a little colour at a time; more can always be added later. If the colour is too dark, add another piece of paste and knead again.

3 To colour a large amount of paste, divide into small pieces, colour each one, then knead all the pieces together to blend.

VILLA FLEUR

The stunning louvred effect on the shutters
is made simply by cutting the sugarpaste
and filling in with icing sugar. Allow a little
extra time to decorate this cake.

Cutting against a metal
ruler, make cuts across
the pale pink section of
the shutters every 5mm
(¼in) to form a louvre
effect, then using a pin
make small holes along
the edge of the blind.

Gently rub over the
cuts and pin holes with
icing (confectioner's)
sugar to fill. Brush
away any excess sugar
and use a smoother to
remove any dents.

*18cm (7in) or 20cm (8in) square cake of
your choice, see pages 6–9*

•

marzipan to cover cake

•

1kg (2lb) sugarpaste

•

*pink, blue, yellow, purple, orange and
green paste food colours*

•

icing (confectioner's) sugar

•

ribbon and candles to decorate, optional

1 Cover the cake with marzipan, see page 10,
then allow to dry in a warm place for 24 hours.
Trace the templates from page 74 onto grease-
proof (parchment) paper, then trim the paper
to fit the cake top.
2 Colour 140g (4½oz) sugarpaste pink, 90g
(3oz) pale pink, 30g (1oz) blue, 30g (1oz) lilac,
30g (1oz) yellow, 15g (½oz) orange, 30g (1oz)
pale green, 15g (½oz) green and set aside 60g
(2oz) white. Roll out the remaining sugarpaste
to 2.5mm (⅛in) and cover the cake, see pages
11–12.
3 Secure tracing A (window) in position on the
cake top, transfer the design then remove the
tracing. Cut out the window and inlay with the
darker shade of pink sugarpaste.
4 Secure tracing B (shutters and window inset)
in position, transfer the design then remove the
tracing. Cut out the shutters and inlay with
pale pink sugarpaste. Cut out the window top

and inlay with pale pink sugarpaste. Cut out
the top panes and inlay with white sugarpaste.
Cut out the top half of the middle panes and
inlay with white sugarpaste to form blinds. Cut
out the lower half of the middle panes and
inlay with pale pink sugarpaste. Cut out the
bottom window panes and inlay with pale pink
sugarpaste. Cutting against a metal ruler, make
cuts every 5mm (¼in) across the pale pink
section of the shutters to form a louvre effect.
Using a pin, make small holes along the edge
of the blinds. Rub over the cuts and pin holes
with icing (confectioner's) sugar to fill.
5 Secure tracing C (flowers and leaves) in
position, transfer the design then remove the
tracing. Cut out the flowers and inlay with
the appropriate coloured sugarpaste, see the
finished photograph for colour guide. Cut out
the leaves and inlay with the appropriate shade
of green sugarpaste. Cut out the flower and
leaves on the window top and inlay with white
sugarpaste.
6 Secure tracing D (lilac and orange flower
centres) in position, transfer the design then
remove the tracing. Cut out the flower centres
and inlay with white sugarpaste. With a pin
head, make small dents in the centre of the
blue flowers and fill with small balls of white
sugarpaste. The yellow flowers can be made
in the same way instead of cutting out and
inlaying.
7 Lightly dust the cake top with icing sugar
and use a smoother to remove any dents.
Decorate with ribbon and candles if using.

LET'S PARTY

A fun cake to celebrate 50 years! You can substitute other numbers (see page 80) and hang the frogs in a similar way.

20cm (8in) or 23cm (9in) square cake of your choice, see pages 6–9

•

marzipan to cover cake

•

875g (1¾lb) sugarpaste

•

pink, green and yellow paste food colours

•

icing (confectioner's) sugar to dust

•

green edible food colour pen

•

ribbon and candles to decorate, optional

1 Cover the cake with marzipan, see page 10, then allow to dry in a warm place for 24 hours. Trace the templates from page 75 onto grease-proof (parchment) paper, then trim the paper to fit the cake top.
2 Colour 185g (6oz) sugarpaste pink, 60g (2oz) with green and yellow mixed together, 30g (1oz) dark green and set aside 60g (2oz) white. Roll out the remaining sugarpaste and cover the cake, see pages 11–12.
3 Secure tracing A (50) in position on the cake top, transfer the design then remove the tracing. Cut out '5' and inlay with pink sugarpaste. Cut out '0' and inlay with pink sugarpaste.
4 Secure tracing B ('0' centre, bottle on '5' and frogs' feet) in position, transfer the design then remove the tracing. Cut out '0' centre and inlay with white sugarpaste. Cut out the bottle on '5' and inlay with dark green sugarpaste. Cut out the frogs' feet and inlay with light green sugarpaste.
5 Secure tracing C (frogs and bottle on '0') in position, transfer the design then remove the tracing. Cut out the frogs and inlay with pale green sugarpaste. Cut out the bottle and inlay with dark green sugarpaste.
6 Hold tracing D (eyes and bottle labels) in position, transfer the design then remove the tracing. Cut out the eyes and inlay with white sugarpaste. Cut out the labels and inlay with pink sugarpaste. Using the head of a pin, make small dents in frogs' eye centres and inlay with small balls of dark green sugarpaste.
7 Lightly dust the cake top with icing (confectioner's) sugar and use a smoother to remove any dents. Allow the sugarpaste to dry for 24–48 hours or until completely dry and will not dent when pressed. Draw in the frogs' mouths with the edible food colour pen, either free-hand or refer to page 17. Decorate if liked.

EASTER FAIR

This attractive Easter time cake will be
popular with children as they will love the
treats in the middle!

*20cm (8in) or 23cm (9in) round cake of
your choice, see pages 6–9*

•

marzipan to cover cake

•

750g (1½lb) sugarpaste

•

*pink, blue, yellow and purple paste food
colours*

•

icing (confectioner's) sugar to dust

•

*three 38cm (15in) lengths each of pink,
blue, yellow and lilac floristry ribbon*

•

125g (4oz) mini chocolate eggs

1 With a 6cm (2½in) plain pastry cutter, mark
and cut out a well in the centre of the cake,
approximately 2.5cm (1in) deep.
2 Roll out the marzipan to cover the cake,
then cut a 3.5cm (1½in) cross in the centre.
Using your hands for support, drape the
marzipan over the cake with the cross placed
in the centre. Ease the cross sections into the
well to cover the sides, then trim away excess
triangles from the bottom of the well. Carefully
ease the marzipan to fit the sides of the cake,
then trim away excess with a sharp knife. Using
the pastry cutter, cut a circle of marzipan to
cover the bottom of the well. Allow to dry in
a warm place for 24 hours.
3 Make four tracings from the bunny template
on page 76 onto greaseproof (parchment)
paper, then trim the paper to fit the cake top.

Colour 30g (1oz) sugarpaste pink, 30g (1oz)
blue, 30g (1oz) yellow and 30g (1oz) lilac. Roll
out the remaining sugarpaste to 2.5mm (⅛in)
and cover the cake following the same procedure as for the marzipan.
4 Secure the bunny tracings in position on the
cake top, transfer the design then remove the
tracings. Cut out each bunny in turn and inlay
with a different coloured sugarpaste.
5 Lightly dust the cake top with icing (confectioner's) sugar and use a smoother to remove
any dents.
6 Tear the ribbons into 2.5mm (⅛in) strips
and curl using the blunt edge of a knife.
Arrange the ribbons so they fall between the
bunnies. Make four 1cm (½in) flat buttons of
sugarpaste, brush one side with cooled boiled
water and use to secure the ribbons to the
bottom of centre well. Fill the well with mini
chocolate eggs.

To create a well in the
cake centre, use a 6cm
(2½in) plain pastry
cutter to mark and cut
the centre of the cake.
Cut across the middle
with a sharp knife then
ease the cut sections
out. Level the bottom
of the well by carefully
scraping away cake
with a spoon.

· TIP ·

For added excitement
for children, place some
cute little Easter chicks
amongst the mini
chocolate eggs.

HALLOWEEN

This dramatic pumpkin and black cat cake
sets the scene for a Halloween get together.

*20cm (8in) or 23cm (9in) round cake of
your choice, see pages 6–9*

•

marzipan to cover cake

•

750g (1½lb) sugarpaste

•

*orange, green, yellow and black paste food
colours*

•

icing (confectioner's) sugar

•

ribbon and candles to decorate, optional

1 Cover the cake with marzipan, see page 10,
then allow to dry in a warm place for 24 hours.
Trace the templates from page 76 onto grease-
proof (parchment) paper, then trim the paper
to fit the cake top.
2 Colour 75g (2½ oz) sugarpaste orange,
7g (¼oz) green, 45g (1½oz) yellow and 45g
(1½oz) black. Roll out the remaining sugarpaste to 2.5mm (⅛in) and cover the cake, see
pages 11–12.
3 Secure tracing A (pumpkin) in position on
the cake top, transfer the design then remove
the tracing. Cut out the pumpkin and inlay
with orange sugarpaste. Cut out the stalk and
inlay with green sugarpaste.
4 Secure tracing B (pumpkin face and cat) in
position, transfer the design then remove the
tracing. Cut out the pumpkin face and inlay
with yellow sugarpaste. Cut out the cat and
inlay with black sugarpaste.
5 Hold tracing C (cat's eyes) in position,
transfer the design then remove the tracing.

Cut out the eyes and inlay with white sugarpaste. Using a cocktail stick (toothpick), make
small dents in the centre of the eyes and fill
with small rolls of orange sugarpaste. Make
small cuts in the centre of the eyes and fill with
rolls of black sugarpaste.
6 Using a modelling knife, cut out a small
triangle for the cat's nose, then make cuts for
whiskers and mouth. Rub over the cuts with
icing (confectioner's) sugar to fill.
7 Lightly dust the cake top with icing sugar
and use a smoother to remove any dents.
Decorate with ribbon and candles if using.

Carefully lay the cat in
position on the cake
top, smooth the tail
into position, then use
a modelling knife to
ease the ears and paws
into place. Gently
smooth over until the
cut edges meet.

· TIP ·

After rubbing icing
(confectioner's) sugar
into the cat's face,
cover with cling film
(plastic wrap) until all
the icing sugar has been
absorbed.

NOEL, NOEL

A really effective Christmas cake design
which is very easy to accomplish. Candles,
placed at the ends of the branches, add the
finishing touch.

*20cm (8in) or 23cm (9in) round cake of
your choice, see pages 6–9*

•

marzipan to cover cake

•

750g (1½lb) sugarpaste

•

green and red paste food colours

•

icing (confectioner's) sugar to dust

•

silver dragees

•

ribbon and candles to decorate, optional

· TIPS ·

To ensure the correct
position of the silver
dragees on the tree, use
a pin head to make
dents in the sugarpaste
then lightly smooth
over with your fingers.
Press the silver dragees
into dents.

When inlaying, put the
points of each tree
section into position
first, then guide the
curved edges into place.

1 Cover the cake with marzipan, see page 10,
then allow to dry in a warm place for 24 hours.
Trace the templates from page 77 onto grease-
proof (parchment) paper, then trim the paper
to fit the cake top.
2 Colour 185g (6oz) sugarpaste dark green,
30g (1oz) red and set aside 15g (½oz) white.
Roll out the remaining sugarpaste to 2.5mm
(⅛in) and cover the cake, see pages 11–12.
3 Secure tracing A (tree and tub) in position
on the cake top, transfer the design then remove
the tracing. Cut out the tree sections and inlay
with dark green sugarpaste. Cut out the tub
and inlay with red sugarpaste.
4 Secure tracing B (bow) in position, transfer
the design then remove the tracing. Cut out the
bow and inlay with white sugarpaste.
5 Lightly dust the cake top with icing (confectioner's) sugar and use a smoother to remove

any dents. Press silver dragees into position on
the tree. Decorate with ribbon and candles if
using.

Cutting out a
Christmas tree section,
working along the
outside edge of the pin
prick marks.

GABRIELLE

For the Christmas cake design with a
difference, make this beautiful angel cake.
Silver dragees are lightly pressed into the
sugarpasted cake surface to create the effect
of sparkling stars.

*20cm (8in) or 23cm (9in) round cake of
your choice, see pages 6–9*

•

marzipan to cover cake

•

875g (1¾lb) sugarpaste

•

blue and yellow paste food colours

•

icing (confectioner's) sugar to dust

•

silver dragees

•

ribbon and candles to decorate, optional

1 Cover the cake with marzipan, see page 10,
then allow to dry in a warm place for 24 hours.
Trace the templates from page 78 onto grease-
proof (parchment) paper, then trim the paper
to fit the cake top.
2 Colour 185g (6oz) sugarpaste dark blue, 90g
(3oz) yellow and set aside 90g (3oz) white. Roll
out the remaining sugarpaste to 2.5mm (⅛in)
and cover the cake, see pages 11–12.
3 Secure the inset tracing in position on the
cake top, transfer the inset outline then remove
the tracing. Cut out the inset and inlay with
dark blue sugarpaste.
4 Secure tracing A in position on the cake top,
transfer the design then remove the tracing.
Cut out and inlay all the yellow sections first
(wing, hair, trumpet and dress sections), then
cut out and inlay all the white sections (halo,

sleeve/hand, remaining dress sections). See the
finished cake photograph for colour guide.
5 Secure tracing B (stripes on sleeve) in position, transfer the design then remove the
tracing. Cut out the stripes and inlay with
yellow sugarpaste.
6 Lightly dust the cake top with icing (confectioner's) sugar and use a smoother to remove
any dents. Press silver dragees into position
around Gabrielle. Decorate with ribbon and
candles if using.

When all the yellow
sections are complete,
cut out each of the
remaining sections in
turn and inlay with
white sugarpaste.

· TIPS ·

If the dark blue
sugarpaste appears
patchy or dry from
using icing
(confectioner's) sugar,
cover with cling film
(plastic wrap) for 1–2
hours or until all the
icing sugar has been
absorbed.

For an easy round cake
inset guide, see the Tip
on page 42.

MR FROSTY

This charming Christmas cake will
appeal to adults and children alike, and add
to the festive cheer.

*18cm (7in) or 20cm (8in) round cake of
your choice, see pages 6–9*

•

marzipan to cover cake

•

750g (1½lb) sugarpaste

•

*blue, green, red and black paste food
colours*

•

icing (confectioner's) sugar to dust

•

black edible food colour pen

•

ribbon and candles to decorate, optional

· TIPS ·

For an easy round cake
inset guide, see the Tip
on page 42.

~

If short of time, omit
the red tree decorations
and decorate with silver
or coloured dragees
instead (see pages 54
and 56).

1 Cover the cake with marzipan, see page 10,
then allow to dry in a warm place for 24 hours.
Trace the templates from page 79 onto grease-
proof (parchment) paper, then trim the paper
to fit the cake top.
2 Colour 155g (5oz) sugarpaste pale blue, 60g
(2oz) green, 60g (2oz) red, 15g (½oz) black
and set aside 60g (2oz) white. Roll out the
remaining sugarpaste to 2.5mm (⅛in) and
cover the cake, see pages 11–12.
3 Secure the inset tracing in position on the
cake top, transfer the inset outline then remove
the tracing. Cut out the inset and inlay with
pale blue sugarpaste.
4 Secure tracing A (Mr Frosty, top hat, tree,
tub) in position on the cake top, transfer the
design then remove the tracing. Cut out Mr
Frosty and inlay with white sugarpaste. Cut
out the top hat and inlay with black sugar-

paste. Cut out the tree and inlay with green
sugarpaste. Cut out the tub and inlay with red
sugarpaste.
5 Secure tracing B (tree decoration, scarf, hat
band, nose and tub bow) in position, transfer
the design then remove the tracing. Cut out the
tree decorations and inlay with red sugarpaste.
Cut out the scarf, nose and hat band and inlay
with red sugarpaste. Cut out the tub bow and
inlay with white sugarpaste. (If you would like
an orange nose on Mr Frosty, add a little
yellow paste colour to some red sugarpaste.)
6 Using the head of a pin, make small holes in
the pale blue sugarpaste to form snowflakes,
then fill with small balls of white sugarpaste.
7 Lightly dust the cake top with icing (confectioner's) sugar and use a smoother to remove
any dents.
8 Allow the sugarpaste to dry for 24–48 hours
or until completely dry and will not dent when
pressed. Use the black edible food colour pen
to draw in Mr Frosty's eyes and mouth.
Decorate with ribbon and candles if using.

Cut the tree tub from
red sugarpaste, cutting
between the two lines
of pin marks. Carefully
lift the tub from red
sugarpaste and inlay
into cake top.

TEMPLATES

Each template is shown by a different coloured line. Make a separate tracing of each template (A, B, C, D) onto greaseproof (parchment) paper using a pencil, then trim off the excess paper to fit the cake top.

When tracing templates B, C and D, it will help to draw registration lines in a different-coloured pen or crayon by tracing sections from the top and bottom of either template A or the previous template. Then, when placing these tracings on the cake top, simply make sure the coloured registration lines are in the correct position over the coloured inlaid sections.

CUDDLES
page 18

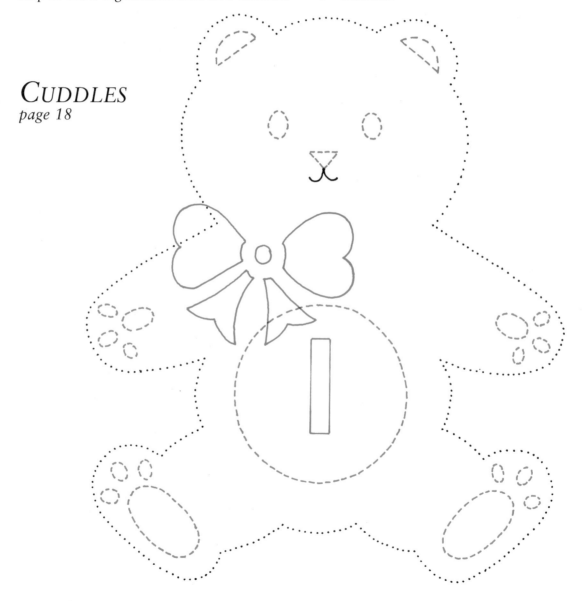

Template A	··············
Template B	– – – – – –
Template C	————
Template D	————
Features to draw	━━━━━

Hetty, betty
AND BABY BOO
page 20

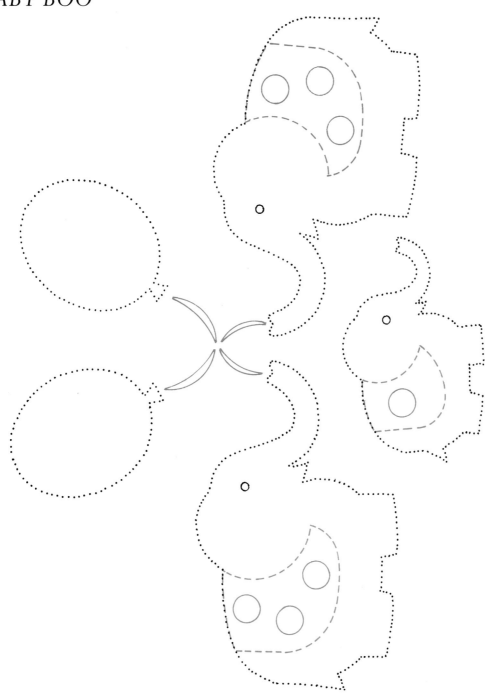

BRULEE
page 22

Template A	....
Template B	- - - - - - - - - - -
Template C	——————
Template D	——————
Features to draw	—————

CAKE TOP INSET

CUTHBERT
page 24

JASPER'S FRIEND
page 26

Template A	··················
Template B	− − − − − −
Template C	——————
Template D	——————
Features to draw	——————

DINO
page 28

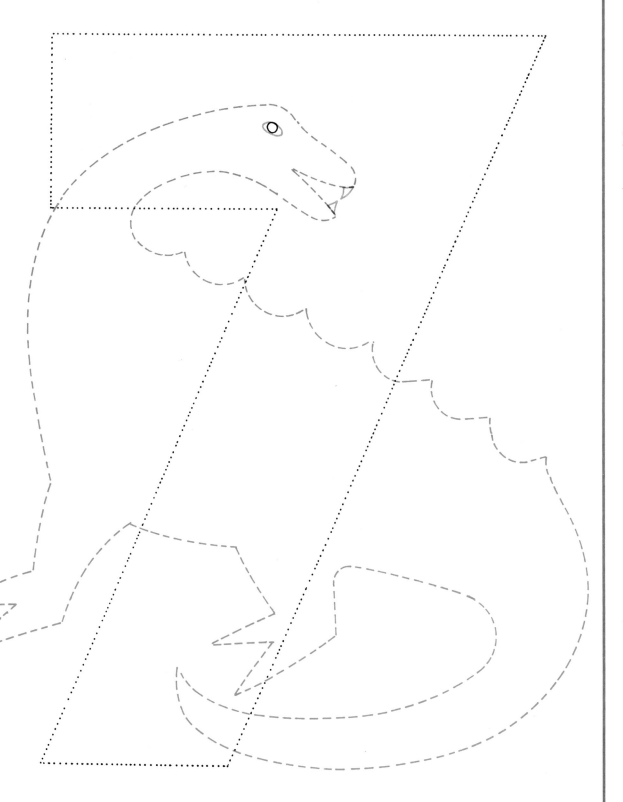

· TEMPLATES ·

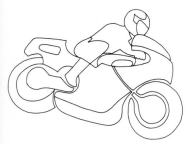

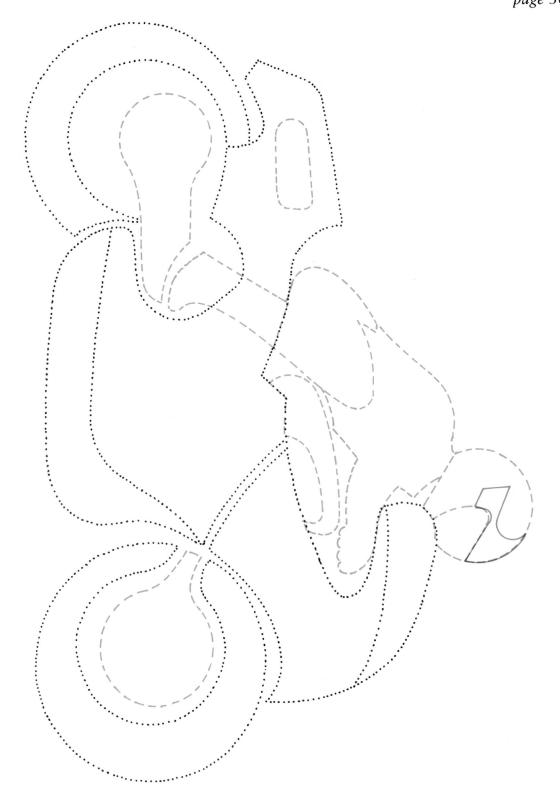

Template A	·············
Template B	− − − − −
Template C	——————
Template D	——————
Features to draw	——————

TEMPLATES

TROJAN CLOUD
page 32

67

CASTAWAY
page 34

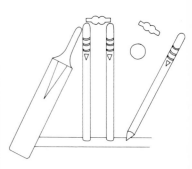

Template A	· · · · · · · · · · · · · · · · · ·
Template B	– – – – – – – – –
Template C	———————
Template D	———————
Features to draw	▬▬▬▬▬▬▬

BOWLED OUT

page 36

CAKE TOP INSET

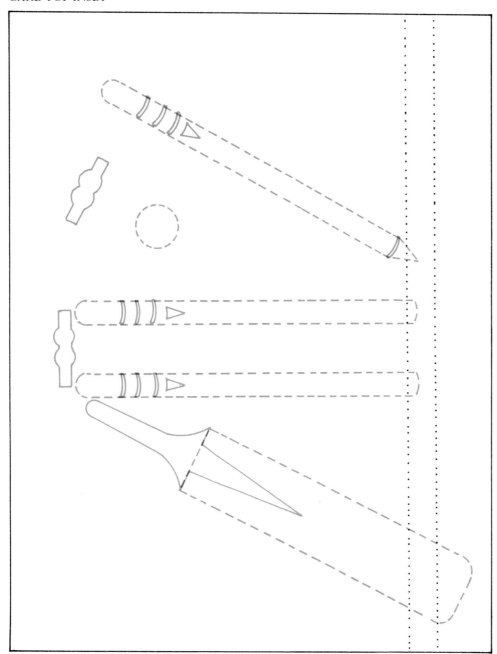

FA CUP
page 38

Template A	····························
Template B	- - - - - - - - - -
Template C	——————————
Template D	——————————
Features to draw	——————————

BOYS' TOY
page 40

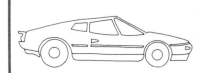

CAKE TOP INSET

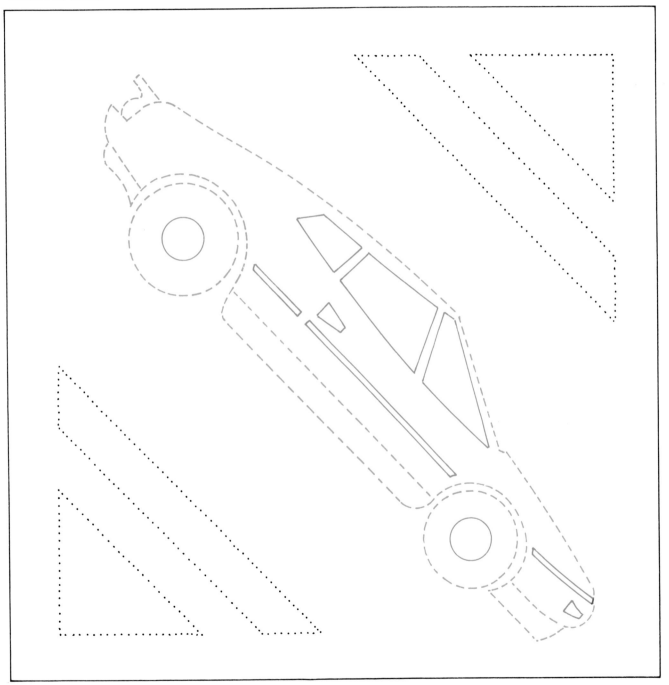

TEE OFF
page 42

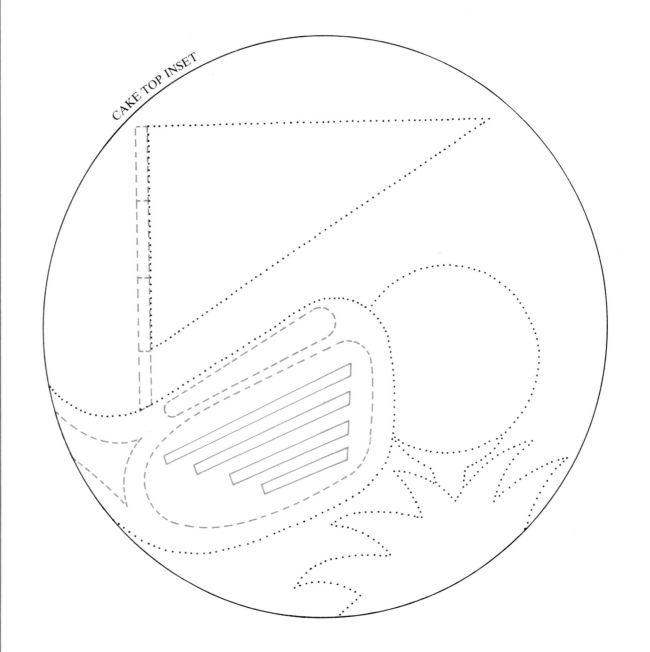

CAKE TOP INSET

Template A	···
Template B	– – – – – – – – – – –
Template C	———————————
Template D	———————————
Features to draw	━━━━━━━━━━

SPRING BOUQUET
page 44

VILLA FLEUR
page 46

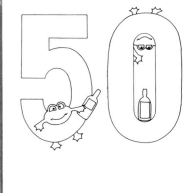

Template A	....
Template B	- - - - - - - - - - - - -
Template C	—————————
Template D	—————————
Features to draw	━━━━━━━

LET'S PARTY
page 48

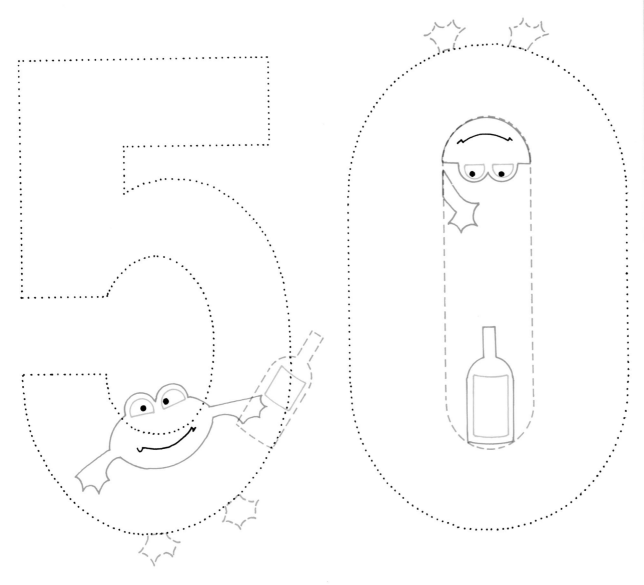

EASTER FAIR
page 50

HALLOWEEN
page 52

Template A	· · · · · · · · · · · ·
Template B	– – – – – – – –
Template C	———————
Template D	———————
Features to draw	━━━━━━━

NOEL, NOEL
page 54

GABRIELLE
page 56

CAKE TOP INSET

Template A	··············
Template B	------
Template C	————
Template D	————
Features to draw	━━━━

MR FROSTY
page 58

CAKE TOP INSET

NUMBERS

Use these numbers as templates when substituting or adding to the cake design. If a larger or smaller number is required, trace off the number shown here onto a sheet of tracing paper or copy paper, using a black felt tip pen to draw the outline. Enlarge or reduce on a suitable photocopier.

1 2 3 4 5

6 7 8 9 0

1 2 3 4 5

6 7 8 9 0

ONE DIRECTION
Fact File Sticker Book

CONTENTS

The talented One Direction boys, Liam, Harry, Zayn, Louis and Niall, have had their dreams of musical stardom skyrocket to almost unimaginable international success.

How could One Direction possibly match their already amazing success? In February 2013, One Direction were honoured with the chance to release the official Comic Relief Charity Single One Way or Another (Teenage Kicks), and performed the single at the 2013 Brit Awards where they won the newly created Global Success Award showcasing their phenomenal international success and stardom.

The same month saw them embark on their second world concert tour, where they tour the globe until October 2013. The tour consists of over 100 shows, selling a jaw dropping 300,000 tickets within a day of release in the UK and Ireland. Along with their yearlong tour, 2013 has seen the release of a 3D biopic film called This Is Us centring on the group which launched in UK cinemas in the summer of 2013.

Harry Styles said in a statement, "You get moments all the time that kind of make you pinch yourself, some of them make you quite emotional. Winning a BRIT was a big moment because we were just so excited to be at the awards in the first place. Selling out Madison Square Garden was pretty amazing too. Then we woke to the news that our UK tour was sold out. It was crazy!".

With their fans as passionate as ever, these ambitious and talented young boys are showing no signs of slowing down. Still eager to turn more of their dreams into reality, we can expect great things from One Direction in the upcoming years!

HARRY

FULL NAME	**Harry Edward Styles**
BORN	1st February 1994
STAR SIGN	Aquarius
EYE COLOUR	Green
HOME TOWN	Holmes Chapel, Cheshire
BROTHERS AND SISTERS	Older Sister (Gemma)
SCHOOL	Holmes Chapel Comprehensive
FIRST CONCERT	Nickleback
BIGGEST FEAR	Harry has Ophidiophobia (a fear of snakes … like Indiana Jones!)
FIRST KISS	A girl at school at age 11
CELEBRITY CRUSHES	Cheryl Cole, Rihanna, Angelina Jolie, Kate Winslet
IDOLS	David Beckham, Elvis Presley
SKILLS	Juggling, Playing the Kazoo, Can speak French, Knitting

Favourites

SUBJECT IN SCHOOL	English
BAND/ARTIST	The Beatles, Adele, Queen, Foster the People, Kings of Leon, Coldplay
FILMS	Love Actually, Titanic, The Notebook
TV SHOW	Family Guy
COLOUR	Orange and Blue
FOOD	Tacos, Sweetcorn, Apple Juice, T.G.I.Fridays, Chocolate HobNobs
AFTERSHAVE	CK In 2U, Diesel Fuel For Life, Bleu de Chanel

LIKES	Long Showers, Tattoos (he has over 30!), Massages, Manchester United
DISLIKES	Mayonnaise, Beetroot, White Cars
PERFECT DATE	Dinner and a movie
IDEAL GIRLFRIEND	Non-smoker / non-swearers who wear pink and don't complain about their weight. Good sense of humour. Blue eyes.
IF HE WASN'T IN 1D	Harry would want to be at university
ONE MAD FACT	Harry bites two Twix bars at the same time because he doesn't want one to feel lonely

LIAM

FULL NAME	**Liam James Payne**
BORN	29th August 1993
STAR SIGN	Virgo
EYE COLOUR	Brown
HOME TOWN	Wolverhampton
BROTHERS AND SISTERS	2 older sisters (Ruth and Nicola)
SCHOOL	Music Technology student at City of Wolverhampton College
FIRST CONCERT	Gareth Gates
BIGGEST FEAR	Spoons
FIRST KISS	11 (a girl named Vicky)
CELEBRITY CRUSHES	Leona Lewis, Miley Cyrus
IDOLS	Justin Timberlake, Gary Barlow
SKILLS	Playing the guitar, Beatboxing

Favourites

SUBJECT IN SCHOOL	P.E and Science
BAND/ARTIST	Jay Z, Kanye West, Ed Sheeran, Passenger, *NSYNC
FILMS	The Toy Story films (He cried watching Toy Story 3 and Marley and Me)
TV SHOW	Friends
COLOUR	Purple
FOOD	Maltesers, Coca Cola, Cheeseburgers
AFTERSHAVE	Paco Rabanne's 1 million

LIKES	Basketball, Cooking, Boxing, Turtles, Tattoos
DISLIKES	Bullies (he used to get bullied at school), Swearing, Burping, Bling
PERFECT DATE	Sitting in the back of a movie theatre or walking in a park
IDEAL GIRLFRIEND	Shy, cheeky girls. Nice eyes. Quiet. Friendly. Curly hair
IF HE WASN'T IN 1D	Liam would want to work in a factory building aeroplanes or become a property developer
ONE MAD FACT	Because of Liam's fear of spoons, he eats ice-cream with a fork

ONE DIRECTION

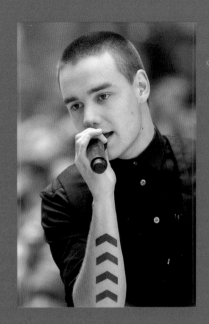

ONE DIRECTION

LOUIS

FULL NAME	**Louis William Tomlinson**
BORN	24 December 1991
STAR SIGN	Capricorn
EYE COLOUR	Blue
HOME TOWN	Doncaster, South Yorkshire
BROTHERS AND SISTERS	5 younger half-sisters (Lottie, Georgia, Felicity, Phoebe and Daisy)
SCHOOL	Hall Cross School
FIRST CONCERT	Busted (Year 6 at school)
BIGGEST FEAR	Birds, Pigeons
FIRST KISS	Year 5 (he can't remember much about it)
CELEBRITY CRUSHES	Natalie Portman
IDOLS	Robbie Williams
SKILLS	Can play the piano

Favourites

SUBJECT IN SCHOOL	Drama
BAND/ARTIST	Ed Sheeran, The Fray, James Morrison, The Killers
FILMS	Grease, Forrest Gump
TV SHOW	Misfits, One Tree Hill
COLOUR	Dark Red
FOOD	Marmite, Pasta, Cookie Dough dessert from Pizza Hut
GROOMING PRODUCT	Dry Shampoo

LIKES	Manchester United, Tennis, Partying, Shoes (Chinos and Toms), Tattoos
DISLIKES	Baked Beans, People who chew their food too loudly, Birds
PERFECT DATE	Going to a theme park
IDEAL GIRLFRIEND	Girls who eat carrots, Girls who wear glasses (real or not), Confident, Good sense of humour
IF HE WASN'T IN 1D	Louis would want to train to be a Drama Teacher
ONE MAD FACT	Louis's band mates say he sleepwalks and apparently he is the messiest of the five

NIALL

FULL NAME	**Niall James Horan**
BORN	13th September 1993
STAR SIGN	Virgo
EYE COLOUR	Blue
HOME TOWN	Mullingar, Westmeath, Ireland
BROTHERS AND SISTERS	Older brother (Greg). He's the only member of One Direction with a brother
SCHOOL	Colaiste Mhuire
FIRST CONCERT	Busted (he was 10)
BIGGEST FEAR	Claustrophobia, Pigeons
FIRST KISS	11 or 12 (a French foreign exchange student)
CELEBRITY CRUSHES	Cheryl Cole, Christine Bleakley, Miranda Cosgrove (iCarly)
IDOLS	Michael Bublé, Justin Bieber (He is a Bieleber), Barack Obama

Favourites

SKILLS	Can play the guitar
SUBJECT IN SCHOOL	Geography and French
BAND/ARTIST	Frank Sinatra, Bon Jovi, Coldplay, Michael Bublé, The Script
FILMS	Grease, Horror Movies, He cried at Finding Nemo
TV SHOW	Two and a Half Men
COLOUR	Green (He also likes Blue)
FOOD	Nando's, Pizza , Japanese, Italian, Chinese, Terry's Chocolate Orange
AFTERSHAVE	Armani Mania

LIKES	Food, Derby County Football Club, Singing in the shower, Giraffes
DISLIKES	The Only Way Is Essex
PERFECT DATE	Something fun and crazy, like going to a theme park
IDEAL GIRLFRIEND	Girls with brown eyes, Shy girls, Girls who can speak different languages and speak in different accents, Intelligent girls, Girls who don't wear make-up
IF HE WASN'T IN 1D	Niall would want to be a sound engineer
ONE MAD FACT	Niall is a natural brunette but has dyed his hair since the age of 12

ZAYN

FULL NAME	**Zayn (Zain) Javadd Malik**
BORN	12th Januaray 1993
STAR SIGN	Capricorn
EYE COLOUR	Hazel
HOME TOWN	East Bowling, Bradford
BROTHERS AND SISTERS	One older sister (Doniya) and two younger sisters (Waliyha and Safaa)
SCHOOL	Tony High School
FIRST CONCERT	JLS
BIGGEST FEAR	Open water, Heights, Clowns
FIRST KISS	A girl named Sophie when he was ten (she was taller than him so he had to stand on a brick to reach her lips)
CELEBRITY CRUSHES	Megan Fox, Jessica Alba, Rihanna
IDOLS	Michael Jackson
SKILLS	Drawing, Acting, Cooking
SUBJECT IN SCHOOL	English, Art and Drama
BAND/ARTIST	Bruno Mars, Chris Brown, Urban Music, ★NSYNC
FILMS	Scarface
TV SHOW	Family Guy
COLOUR	Electric Blue and Red
FOOD	Chicken, Nando's, Red Bull, Samosas, Spaghetti Bolognese
ATFTERSHAVE	Unforgivable by Sean John
LIKES	Harry Potter, Reading, Lions, Manchester United, Tattoos
DISLIKES	People who chew loudly, Messiness
PERFECT DATE	Going out for a meal, the cinema and home to chill with some drinks
IDEAL GIRLFRIEND	Zayn is very attracted to girls' eyes (whatever the colour), Intelligent girls, Someone he can spoil, Curvy girls, Girls who play hard to get
IF HE WASN'T IN 1D	Zayn would want to be an English teacher
ONE MAD FACT	Zayn has a strange pre-gig superstition – brushing his teeth before going on stage

(Favourites)

15